7

GaNdHi

GandHi

by Diane Bailey

Illustrated by Charlotte Ager

Editor Allison Singer
Senior Editor Lizzie Davey
Senior Designer Joanne Clark

Project Editor Roohi Sehgal
Additional Editorial Jolyon Goddard, Kritika Gupta
Project Art Editor Yamini Panwar
Senior Art Editor Nidhi Mehra
Jacket Coordinator Francesca Young
Jacket Designer Joanne Clark
Senior DTP Designer Neeraj Bhatia
DTP Designer Sachin Gupta
Picture Researcher Aditya Katyal
Illustrator Charlotte Ager
Senior Producer, Pre-Production Nikoleta Parasaki
Producer Basia Ossowska
Managing Editors Laura Gilbert, Monica Saigal
Deputy Managing Art Editor Ivy Sengupta
Managing Art Editor Diane Peyton Jones
Delhi Team Head Malavika Talukder
Creative Director Helen Senior
Publishing Director Sarah Larter

Subject Consultant Priti Mishra
Literacy Consultant Stephanie Laird

First American Edition, 2019
Published in the United States by DK Publishing
345 Hudson Street, New York, New York 10014

Copyright © 2019 Dorling Kindersley Limited
DK, a Division of Penguin Random House LLC
19 20 21 22 23 10 9 8 7 6 5 4 3 2 1
001–311453–Jan/19

A catalog record for this book is available from the Library of Congress.
ISBN: 978-1-4654-7842-9 (Paperback)
ISBN: 978-1-4654-7463-6 (Hardcover)

DK books are available at special discounts when purchased in bulk for sales promotions,
premiums, fund-raising, or educational use. For details, contact:
DK Publishing Special Markets,
345 Hudson Street, New York, New York 10014
SpecialSales@dk.com

Printed and bound in China

A WORLD OF IDEAS:
SEE ALL THERE IS TO KNOW

www.dk.com

Dear Reader,

If you saw a picture of Gandhi and didn't know who he was, you might think he's just a guy in glasses and sandals, sitting at a spinning wheel. When you learned what he had done, you might think, **Really**?

On the outside, Gandhi wasn't very big or strong. He was smart enough, but no genius. He didn't have a big bank account, and—at least at first—he wasn't friends with a lot of powerful people. He was about as ordinary as they come. But he knew that, and he took advantage of it.

Gandhi had the willpower to stay true to his beliefs and carry out his plans even when it seemed like everything was working against him. Everything he did, no matter how small, was a step forward. If he didn't act, who would? And when he acted, people followed him.

His life showed that the "ordinary," multiplied a million times over, isn't ordinary anymore. It's extraordinary.

Diane Bailey

The life of... GANDHI

A big heart

As a boy, Mohandas Gandhi was taught to be kind and fair. Later in life, his sense of right and wrong would help him change India.

When Mohandas Gandhi was 12 years old, a man came to his classroom in India. He was there to inspect the school and make sure the students were learning properly. He tested them by reading out a list of English words for them to spell. Mohandas had just started studying English, and he wasn't very good at it yet. He misspelled the word "kettle." Worse, he was the only one in the class who got it wrong.

The regular teacher saw Mohandas's mistake, but the inspector had not yet noticed. There was still time to fix it. The teacher told Mohandas to copy the word correctly from the boy sitting next to him. Mohandas refused. That would be cheating! The teacher was furious. Now he would look bad in front of the inspector—and it was all because of Mohandas's sense of right and wrong.

A class in progress at Mohandas Gandhi's school.

Mohandas was born on October 2, 1869, in Porbandar, a town in western India. He was the youngest in the family. He also had a sister, Raliatbehn; two brothers, Laxmidas and Karsandas; and two half sisters from his father's first marriage.

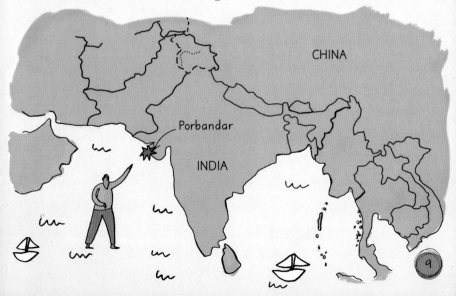

Putlibai and Karamchand
Gandhi, Mohandas's parents.

Honesty and honor were important qualities in Mohandas's family. He said his dad, Karamchand, was "short-tempered," but Mohandas admired that he was loyal and fair. His mother, Putlibai, was such a good person, he called her a saint.

Mohandas was a shy boy, and he was self-conscious about his big ears. After school each day, he ran home so he did not have to talk to the other children. He was more comfortable being with his sister. Mohandas liked the game gilli danda, but otherwise he

GILLI DANDA

One of Gandhi's favorite games was gilli danda, which is a little like baseball. Players use a long stick to hit a peg, then try to run to a set point before their opponent can get the peg back.

wasn't very good at sports. In school, he was an average student who particularly struggled with multiplication tables.

Mohandas Gandhi at seven years old.

Most importantly, however, Mohandas had a big heart. He liked to take care of animals. He even took care of trees! One time, his sister found him high in a mango tree. He'd climbed up to wrap bandages around the pieces of fruit to protect them.

Still, Mohandas had his faults. As part of their Hindu religion, the Gandhi family did not eat meat. Mohandas wanted to try it, so he did—but he didn't tell his parents. He also stole money to buy cigarettes. Another time, he took statues from the local temple to use as props in a game.

What is a temple?   A place for religious worship.

In every case, remorse got the better of him. He admitted what he'd done and took whatever punishment was handed out.

Gandhi's family belonged to the Vaishya caste, for merchants and traders. Generations before, the Gandhis had been grocers. But those days had passed, and now Mohandas's father worked as a government official. Someday, his family hoped, Mohandas would do the same.

Karamchand's job did not make the Gandhis rich, but they had enough money to hire a servant, a boy named Uka.

Uka was not a member of any caste. Like millions of other Indians, he was considered an "untouchable." Untouchables had no status in society. They did the worst jobs, such as sweeping and cleaning toilets, and were shunned by people who belonged to the castes.

One day, Putlibai found out Mohandas had accidentally touched Uka. She told him to wash himself thoroughly. It was the only

THE CASTE SYSTEM

In the Hindu religion, people were born into a certain group called a caste. Traditionally people in higher castes had more status and respect than those in lower ones. The top caste were the Brahmin, made up of priests and scholars. Next came the Kshatriya, who were soldiers and royalty. Gandhi's family was part of the Vaishya caste of merchants and tradespeople. The lowest caste, the Sudra, were general workers. Some people did not belong to any caste at all. They were *Dalit*, or untouchable, and shunned by everyone else. Discrimination by caste is now illegal in India, although its effects have not disappeared entirely.

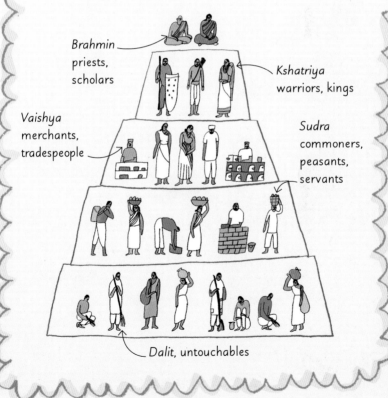

Brahmin
priests,
scholars

Kshatriya
warriors, kings

Vaishya
merchants,
tradespeople

Sudra
commoners,
peasants,
servants

Dalit, untouchables

way to purify himself. Mohandas loved his mother, but he felt she was wrong to think of Uka as dirty. In Mohandas's mind, Uka was no better or worse than anyone else.

In 1883, when Mohandas was 13, he married a neighbor girl named Kasturba. Mohandas did not really want to get married, but the children's parents had arranged it years before.

DID YOU KNOW?

Mohandas was afraid of ghosts, snakes, thieves, and the dark. As a kid, he always slept with a light on.

In 1888, six years later, the couple welcomed a son and named him Harilal. Mohandas, now 19 years old, knew he needed to find a way to support his growing family.

Mohandas with his new wife, Kasturba, on their wedding day in 1883.

Life IN London

As a child, his family had called him by the nickname "Mohania." As an adult, he was known to some by his last name: Gandhi.

In September 1888, Gandhi boarded a ship in Bombay, India, with his suitcase and some money. Kasturba did not like the idea of her husband leaving for England, but he had made up his mind—he was going to London to study law. In three years, when he had finished his studies, he could return to India to work as a lawyer. Then, a few years later, he could find a nice job as a government official, just like his father and grandfather.

That was the plan, anyway. Many of Gandhi's family and friends thought it was a bad one. For starters, it was against Hindu beliefs to travel overseas. Gandhi's mother was worried for another reason, too.

An important part of the Hindu religion is to not hurt other living creatures, including animals. To do that, many Hindus are vegetarians and do not eat any meat, chicken, or fish (although it is not required). Some also avoid animal products, such as milk, cheese, and eggs. The Gandhis were vegetarian, and Gandhi's mother worried that her son might start eating meat if he was surrounded by Englishmen. Gandhi promised his mother that he would stay true to his faith.

THE BRITISH IN INDIA

The British had controlled parts of India for a long time. First the English East India Company took over the Indian market. Then, after an Indian rebellion in 1857, the British government started ruling areas of India directly.

As soon as Gandhi stepped off the ship in England, he realized he did not fit in. He had dressed in a white suit, which he thought would be perfect for the early fall weather. Instead, it was terribly cold, and Gandhi was embarrassed to see all the men around him wearing dark suits.

There were other problems, too. Gandhi didn't speak English well. He didn't know how to use knives and forks, and there wasn't much to eat for a vegetarian. Everyone around him ate meat. For weeks, Gandhi swallowed the few mushy, tasteless vegetables that came with his meals and stuffed the rest of his stomach with bread. He was overjoyed when he finally found a restaurant that served delicious, filling vegetarian food.

Except for his diet, Gandhi tried hard to fit in. He bought fancy suits, gloves, and a top hat to wear, like Englishmen. He fussed over his hair. He took lessons in violin, dancing, and speech. It all cost a fortune. Gandhi was spending his money too fast, and he was no more "English" than when he had started. Finally he gave up, except for trying to learn the language. Gandhi's native language was Gujarati, and he also spoke Hindi. But not many people in London understood those, so Gandhi quickly learned to speak better English. He picked up some French, too.

Gandhi also took a hard look at his finances to see how he could save money. He started eating oatmeal and cocoa for breakfast, and he stuck to eating at a restaurant only at lunchtime. He also bought a stove for his room and learned to cook his own food.

DID YOU KNOW?

After Gandhi learned to cook, carrot soup became one of his favorite things to make.

While he learned in school, Gandhi was also learning some things about himself. He thought a vegetarian diet was important not only for religious reasons, but also for good health. He joined a society for vegetarians to learn more, and often wrote articles for the group's newspaper. He also found that living simply saved money and made him just as content.

Gandhi poses with members of the London Vegetarian Society in 1890.

STAYING CURRENT

In India, Gandhi had never read newspapers, but he loved reading them during his years in London. Besides the vegetarian society's newspaper, he regularly read the *Daily News*, the *Pall Mall Gazette*, and the *Daily Telegraph*.

Gandhi earned his law degree in 1891 and returned to India, where he was happy to be reunited with Kasturba. Their second son, Manilal, was born in 1892. Soon Gandhi got his first case as a lawyer. He had to appear in court with his client, but found that he was tongue-tied! His shy personality had taken over, and he couldn't utter a word in front of the judge. Shamed, Gandhi gave the case to another lawyer.

Even if Gandhi had been a good lawyer, though, building up a successful practice in India could take years. It would be a long time before he would make much money.

A photo of Gandhi taken while he was in London, in 1890.

Fortunately a new opportunity came up that was better for him. Many Indians lived in South Africa, a country at the southern tip of Africa. A company there needed someone who knew the law, but it was equally important to speak English and to understand Indian culture. It was a good fit for Gandhi's skills. Plus, it would only be for a year. In 1893, Gandhi once again said good-bye to Kasturba and boarded a ship—this time, to South Africa.

Chapter 3

Into THE spotlight

As an Indian in South Africa, Gandhi was treated badly by white people. Because of this, he fought for Indians to get more rights.

Gandhi faced a troubling situation in South Africa. At the time, it was ruled by the British and the Dutch. All of the rulers were white, and they looked down on native Africans and immigrants from India and China who had moved to South Africa to find jobs.

Gandhi was Indian, which made him a target for prejudice. The white South Africans who were in charge treated him badly because of the color of his skin, before they had even spoken to him.

What is an immigrant? Someone who moves from their home country to another one, often looking for work.

24

A few days after he arrived in South Africa, Gandhi's new boss took him to a courtroom so he could see how things worked. Gandhi was smartly dressed for work, in a suit and tie. He also wore a traditional cloth turban wrapped around his head.

The British judge gave Gandhi a strange look and asked him to take off the turban. Gandhi knew he looked different, but he did not think there was a good reason to remove his turban. He refused and walked out of the courtroom.

Later, Gandhi's boss sent him on a trip. Gandhi bought a ticket for the first-class car on the train. It cost more, but first class was much more comfortable. He was surprised when the conductor told him he had to move to the third-class section. Another passenger had complained that first class was only for white people. Again, Gandhi would not be pushed around. He refused to change cars. The conductor got a policeman. Together, they forced Gandhi off the train.

After getting kicked off the train, Gandhi spent a cold, sleepless night in the train station. Was this what life in South Africa was like? That night, Gandhi thought hard about his choices—should he fight for his rights or go back to India? He decided to stay. Maybe he could fight back.

While living in South Africa, Gandhi noticed more ways that Indians were treated unfairly. They had to pay high taxes. In some places, they could not own property or vote.

SOUTH AFRICA

In Gandhi's time there, South Africa was split into four regions. The British governed Cape Colony and Natal. The Dutch controlled the Transvaal and Orange Free State. These white, European rulers treated other people poorly and restricted their rights. Black native Africans and Chinese and Indian immigrants had fewer rights than the whites. They also had worse jobs and were not allowed the same freedoms as white people.

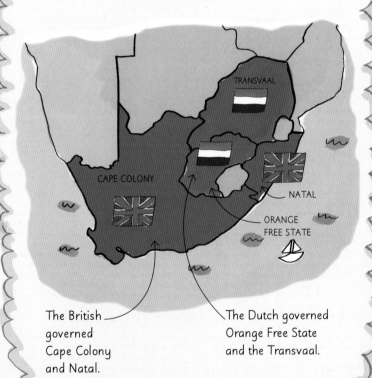

TRANSVAAL

CAPE COLONY

NATAL

ORANGE
FREE STATE

The British
governed
Cape Colony
and Natal.

The Dutch governed
Orange Free State
and the Transvaal.

Indians were not even allowed to walk on the footpaths through the towns—those were reserved for white people. Many white people wanted to shut down Indian businesses, which would leave Indians with no way to make a living. Then they would have to leave the country.

Gandhi protested this unfairness. He gave speeches and wrote letters to newspapers. Other Indians in South Africa saw him as a role model and leader. In 1894, after Gandhi had been in South Africa for a year, his job as a lawyer ended. He got ready to go back to India, but his friends in South Africa begged him to stay. They wanted him to keep working for rights for Indians. Gandhi agreed, and three years later, his family moved to South Africa to be with him.

Over the next several years, Gandhi became even more outspoken as he worked on getting rights for Indians in South Africa. He formed a political group called the Natal Indian Congress. The group would give Indians an organized way to be involved with politics.

Gandhi said the work he did in politics was a "public service." He refused to be paid for it. He did accept money for work as a lawyer, though, so he could take care of his family. His supporters were happy to bring business his way.

This is Gandhi.

Gandhi and the other members of the Natal Indian Congress in 1894.

Even though Gandhi was frustrated with British discrimination against Indians, he felt loyal to the country. In 1899, Britain fought a war against Dutch settlers who also lived in South Africa. Gandhi helped by forming a group of Indians who carried wounded soldiers on stretchers from the battlefields to the hospitals. Gandhi wanted to prove that Indians were brave, loyal people.

In 1903, Gandhi helped start a newspaper in South Africa. It was called the *Indian Opinion*. The newspaper helped him reach even more people. Gandhi felt deeply about his beliefs, and he was not afraid to be in the spotlight. The struggles Indians faced were about to get worse, but Gandhi was ready.

This photograph of Gandhi was taken during his time in South Africa.

4

A simple life

While in South Africa, Gandhi developed ideas about how to live a better life. One thing he felt strongly about was to always behave peacefully.

One day in 1904, Gandhi sat on a train with his nose in a book. He read for hours. By the time he finished his journey, he'd read all night and finished the whole book. The author had written about how people did not need a lot of money or possessions to be happy. This philosophy made sense to Gandhi—and the book gave him an idea.

He decided to start an ashram, a place where he and his followers could live together and focus on a spiritual life. Gandhi bought a piece of property he thought would work. It had some fruit trees and a few buildings. (It also had a lot of snakes.) There was plenty of room for everyone. Several years later, Gandhi started another ashram. People on both of the ashrams worked for themselves and didn't own much. They took care of one another and didn't depend on outsiders. Gandhi thought this was all part of having personal spiritual freedom.

LIFE ON THE ASHRAM

Days on the ashram began early in the morning with reading and prayers. People ate plain meals of porridge, rice, and vegetables. They dressed in simple clothes and did as much as they could for themselves. Gandhi bought a hand mill to grind flour to make his own bread. He also learned to make sandals, so he wouldn't need to buy shoes.

Gandhi continued his political work from the ashrams. In 1906, a new law required Indians living in South Africa to register their names with the government. They had to get a special document and have their fingerprints taken, and they could not move freely around the country. Gandhi thought the law treated Indians like criminals, even though they had not done anything wrong. He refused to obey the law and encouraged other people to do the same. In 1908, he was arrested. Thousands of Indians followed his lead and went to jail, too.

Gandhi was not afraid to go to jail. He believed it was important to stand up for what was right. But he also felt strongly about doing it in a passive, peaceful way.

Gandhi was guided by two philosophies. One was ahimsa, an ancient Hindu belief that people should not behave violently. The other philosophy was satyagraha. Gandhi came up with this idea himself. It means "truth force" or "firmness through truth." For Gandhi, the "truth" was doing the right thing. He was ready to suffer if he had to, because it would show strength and that he believed in his own actions. By showing "firmness," he hoped to convince others that his cause was good.

WHAT'S THE WORD?

Gandhi started practicing satyagraha before there was a word for it. He held a competition in the *Indian Opinion* newspaper to come up with one. One reader suggested "sadagraha," or "firmness in a good cause." Gandhi changed it to mean "firmness through truth."

Over the next few years, the restrictions on Indians got worse. In 1913, the courts ruled that only Christian marriages were legal. That left out almost all Indians, who were Hindus or Muslims.

The British government also said that workers had to pay an annual tax just to be in the country. Most workers could not afford it. The government hoped this would force Indians and other immigrants to leave the country. That way they could keep South Africa "white." The tax inspired more people, especially immigrants, to join Gandhi's movement. In 1913, thousands of coal miners went on strike. They stopped

working, and refused to go back to work until the annual tax was removed.

As they were not working, though, the strikers were not earning money. Gandhi made a brave move. He invited 4,000 strikers to live with him. Gandhi could only afford to give them a pound and a half of bread each day, and an ounce of sugar, but it was better than nothing.

All of South Africa was watching to see what he would do next. Knowing he had everyone's attention, Gandhi led the strikers on a march through the country to protest the unfair laws.

In 1913, Gandhi leads thousands of strikers on a march.

Finally, the government offered a compromise. They agreed to make all marriages legal. They also agreed to remove the annual tax. However, Indians still had to register with the government, and they could not move freely around the country.

Gandhi accepted the offer. He felt he had done all he could. By now, he had spent more than two decades in South Africa. He still wanted to fight for freedom from British rule, but it was time to move the battle. In 1915, he returned to India.

Kasturba and Mohandas just after their return to India in 1915.

This is Gandhi.

A reception for Mohandas and Kasturba in Gujarat, India, on January 27, 1915.

Chapter **5**

Voice OF THE people

In India, Gandhi did the same type of work as in South Africa. He fought for better rights and fairer laws for all people.

Gandhi had big ideas for his homeland, but he'd been away a long time. He needed to get to know his country and its people again. When he got back, he spent a year traveling around, reaching out to ordinary citizens. Often he traveled in third-class train cars. They were crowded and dirty. The food was covered in flies. Gandhi could afford to buy a better ticket, but he wanted to see how most people lived.

Like South Africa, India was governed by the British. Indians could make some decisions for themselves, but mostly the British were in charge. Gandhi thought it was time for this to end. He began spreading his message all over India.

For Gandhi, independence did not just mean taking power from the British—it meant that Indians should find their own personal power and freedom. He encouraged people to work for themselves, not for big businesses. Most large industries were centered in India's big cities. Gandhi wanted to make villages and rural areas stronger.

OLD WAYS, NEW WAYS

Gandhi disliked many things about modern civilization, such as railroads, telephones, and even hospitals. Instead, he wanted to focus on simple, rural living. Some people disagreed. They thought that technology was important to the future, and that India should not get left behind.

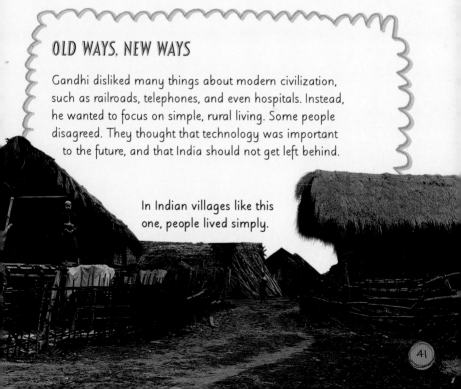

In Indian villages like this one, people lived simply.

41

"If the villages perish, India will perish too."

Gandhi, 1936

With stronger villages, there would be a job for everyone who needed one. Everyone would learn to read and write. There would be clean water and enough food to go around. "If the villages perish, India will perish too," Gandhi warned.

Another part of making a strong country was for all Indians to accept one another. Most Indians were Hindus, and a minority were Muslims. Muslims sometimes felt oppressed by Hindus. Gandhi believed they could solve their problems if both sides worked together. He also said that if Muslims were worried about something, then Hindus should be concerned, too. They had to support each other. This attitude gained him support among Muslims.

RELIGIOUS DIFFERENCES

Hindus and Muslims practiced their faiths differently, and sometimes they got in the way of each other. Hindus did not eat beef, and were offended when Muslims did. Muslims did not like when loud music from Hindu ceremonies would play when they were trying to pray. These issues caused tension between them.

Symbol of
Hinduism

Symbol of
Islam

One group of India's people were treated worse than anyone else. The untouchables were not allowed to mix with the rest of society. Gandhi objected to that. He thought they should be treated like everyone else.

Gandhi had started a new ashram in Sabarmati, India. One day, an untouchable family showed up needing a place to live. Gandhi took them in. A lot of people were horrified and wanted them to leave, but Gandhi stuck to his beliefs and said the untouchables could stay. Eventually the other people accepted the family.

In South Africa, Gandhi had been able to help workers fight back against an unfair government. Now, in India, people again looked to him for his help. One day in 1917, a man asked Gandhi to visit his town, called Champaran.

There, landowners rented land to farmers and forced them to grow indigo, a type of plant used to make blue dye. The farmers did not like it, but they had no choice. Then the price of indigo went down, and the owners raised the farmers' rent to make up the difference. Now the farmers were really in trouble. They could not afford the extra money. They could not even afford to feed their families.

Gandhi visited the region and listened to the farmers' problems. The government knew the landowners were being unfair. They also knew that soon, the whole world would know about it. Gandhi would make sure of that.

With Gandhi's help, the people of Champaran convinced the government to pass a new law that lowered rents and said farmers did not have to grow indigo anymore.

Gandhi took up another cause in 1918 when workers at a textile mill needed a raise to keep up with higher prices. Their bosses had refused the workers' request, and the two sides were in a standoff—until Gandhi made a bold move. He announced he would fast to show his support for the workers. It worked! The bosses gave in and gave the workers a raise.

Gandhi's voice wasn't very loud, but he wasn't afraid to speak out. He had proved himself to be someone who cared for people. It was no wonder that he had gained a title of great respect—now people were calling him Mahatma. It meant someone with a "great soul."

what is a fast? The act of not eating for a period of time, sometimes as a protest against something.

This picture of Gandhi is from 1918, the year he helped the textile workers.

Chapter 6

Farmer AND weaver

Gandhi refused to cooperate with the British government, and he encouraged other people in India not to, as well.

Three hundred million people lived in India. Together, they had a lot to say. Much of it was about the British—and it wasn't positive. The British knew they were outnumbered, and it made them nervous.

In 1919, they passed the Rowlatt Acts. These laws put strict limits on what Indians could say about the government. Anyone who broke the law could get sent to jail without even getting a trial. The British were afraid that if enough Indians protested and banded together, they might overthrow the government. The idea behind the Rowlatt Acts was to scare Indians into keeping quiet.

A lot of people *were* scared—but Gandhi wasn't one of them. When he heard about the new laws, he called for a nationwide hartal. This was a time when Indians would not go to school or work. Instead, they would fast and pray to bring attention to their cause. In most places, the hartal succeeded. Businesses stayed closed, and crowds of thousands came together and held hands to show their unity.

Unfortunately, things had turned violent in some places. In the town of Amritsar, several thousand Indians had gathered in a public square. They did not know that the British military general in charge of the town had made it illegal for Indians to gather. He ordered the police to shoot into the crowd, and almost 400 people were killed.

Gandhi was horrified. The killings convinced him he needed to take stronger action. For years he had tried to cooperate with the British. Now, he settled on the opposite idea: non-cooperation.

When he first arrived in India, Gandhi joined a political group called the Indian National Congress (INC). He helped make it into a group that represented all Indian people, not just rich or powerful ones.

Now he convinced the INC to support non-cooperation. The movement began in August 1920. The idea was to hold a boycott of anything

---

What is a boycott?

Refusing to buy products or use the services of a company or government, usually as a way to protest their actions.

British. People did not vote in elections. Lawyers refused to argue their cases in British courtrooms. Students stayed home from British-run schools.

An important part of the movement was for people to stop buying British products, such as clothing. Gandhi wanted Indians to start making their own clothes. He encouraged everyone in the country to start spinning yarn. Then they could weave homespun cloth called khadi. Gandhi led the way by buying a spinning wheel and spinning for an hour or so each day.

Gandhi spins yarn on a machine specially made for the task.

51

Instead of shirts and pants, Gandhi started wearing a dhoti, a simple cloth wrapped around his waist. He also encouraged people to throw away any clothes that had not been made in India. In 1921, volunteers collected pants, shirts, and hats and put them in a huge pile. Gandhi himself lit the match to burn all of the clothes in a bonfire.

Gandhi hoped that the people's non-cooperation would destroy the British economy in India. Then they would lose their grip on the country and be forced to give India its independence. If his plan did not work, Gandhi was ready to take things up a notch by encouraging people to protest by purposely breaking the

law, such as by not paying their taxes. This type of non-violent protest is called civil disobedience.

One of Gandhi's most important rules for all protests was that things must never become violent. However, not everyone shared his peaceful beliefs. In 1922, a group of protesters turned against the police and killed many of them. Just as with Amritsar a few years earlier, Gandhi was shocked and horrified. He called off his plan for civil disobedience. To him, the movement had to be done peacefully, or it wouldn't be done at all.

Government officials took notice when Gandhi backed down. They believed that it was a sign Gandhi was losing power and influence over the people of India. Here was their chance to stop him. In 1922, the police arrested him for sedition. This time, it would be six years in jail.

When filling out his paperwork at court, Gandhi listed his profession as "farmer and weaver." Everyone knew he was much more than that, though. He was a national hero, willing to go to jail for what was right.

what is sedition?

The act of working against or trying to overthrow the government.

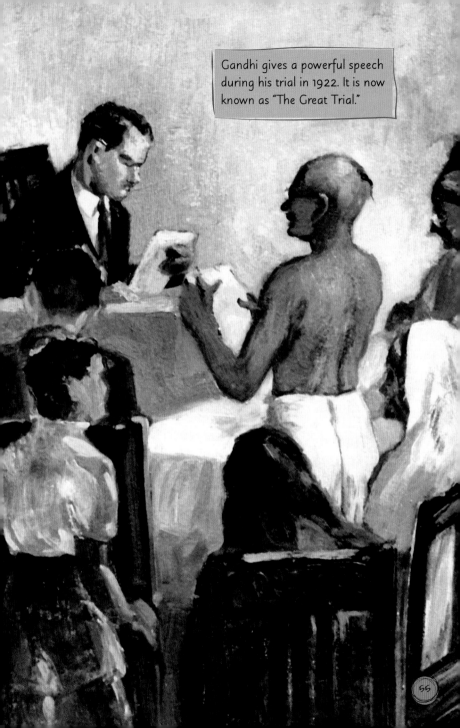

Gandhi gives a powerful speech during his trial in 1922. It is now known as "The Great Trial."

Chapter 7

A new plan

Although the non-cooperation movement had not succeeded, Gandhi did not give up. He put a new plan in place.

Gandhi did not find life in prison too bad. He got up at four in the morning and went to bed at 10 each night. At first the guards took away his spinning wheel, but when Gandhi threatened to go on a hunger strike without it, they gave it back. Gandhi spent several hours each day spinning. He also had plenty of time to read, and he exercised by walking around in the prison courtyard.

One night in January 1924, Gandhi felt sharp pain in his abdomen. Soon he was on his way to the hospital for an operation on his appendix. The surgery went well, but Gandhi was very weak. British officials knew it was risky to send him back to prison. If he died there, he would become a martyr. There would probably be a full revolt from the Indian people. The best option was to let him out.

Gandhi had a lot of work to do. During his two years in prison, the non-cooperation movement had been forgotten. People had put away their spinning wheels and returned to their old ways, and relations between Hindus and Muslims were worse than ever. There were many more Hindus than Muslims. If the British left India, Muslims worried that Hindus would take over, and that the Muslims wouldn't have a say in how the country was run. Maybe it would be better if things stayed the way they were.

Gandhi had his operation at the Sassoon General Hospital in Pune, India.

DID YOU KNOW?

Gandhi talked a lot, but not on Mondays unless it was urgent. He'd taken a vow to stay silent on that day.

There was no clear path forward. Gandhi found it hard to get his message out, but he did not give up. He took a trip all over the country trying to get things back on course. He worked to get people back to making their own khadi, and he continued to speak up for the untouchables. He fasted as a way to show he was committed to peace between Hindus and Muslims.

Indians did not agree on how to be governed. Some wanted full independence from the British. Others thought it would be better to have home rule and stay in the British empire, but with a new constitution that gave people more rights. The constitution would also lay out how the government would be run.

In 1928, Gandhi suggested a plan. It gave Britain one year to come up with a deal to keep India in its empire. If India did not accept the deal, Indians would push for full independence.

"Our non-cooperation has taken the form of non-cooperation ... with each other instead of with the government."

Gandhi,
Young India newspaper,
c. 1924

FAMILY STRUGGLES

Gandhi's four sons and his wife, Kasturba, sometimes became frustrated with him. Gandhi always had time for other people, but he often put his own family last. He also expected more of his family than of anyone else. If they did something wrong, he would scold them in front of everyone! It caused family arguments and tension.

Throughout 1929, India waited. The deadline came and went, with no offer from the British. Now Gandhi had to come up with a new plan. Before he had gone to prison, Gandhi had been thinking about starting a movement of civil disobedience, but he had called it off when things became violent. He decided that it was the right time to try again. The only question was how.

Gandhi needed something that would get the attention of the British. It also had to be something that would be meaningful for the people of India—something simple yet powerful, something every Indian in the country could relate to. But what? "I am furiously thinking night and day," Gandhi told a friend in the early months of 1930.

Finally, the answer came to him.

8

The Salt March

In his greatest act of civil disobedience, Gandhi grabbed the world's attention.

Salt. It was one of the most basic things around. Everyone knew what salt was, and everyone knew why it was important. All people need to eat some salt because it helps hold water in the body. In India's hot climate, people sweated a lot, causing them to lose salt from their bodies. Then they had to buy more—and it was expensive.

The British had put a high tax on salt, and it hit India's poor people especially hard. Even worse, the government had made it illegal to harvest sea salt. For centuries, people in India had taken salt from the salt flats near the ocean's coasts. It was simple and free, until it was outlawed by the British. Most Indians thought that the law was unfair, but what could they do? Gandhi had an idea. He suggested that they could break the law—and they could make a big deal about it.

Gandhi was a showman, and he was about to put on the performance of a lifetime. His plan was incredibly simple. All he was going to do was take salt from the sea.

Salt flats are crusty layers of salt that form gradually where ocean tides wash up on the beach.

Gandhi would not try to break the law in secret, and he would not try to avoid getting caught. Instead, he would do the opposite. He announced his plan far in advance. He wanted the government to know all about it.

On March 12, 1930, Gandhi got up early in the morning, and so did 78 of his followers. They had a long walk in front of them. At 6 a.m., they set off from Gandhi's ashram in Sabarmati to march to Dandi, a village in western India on the coast of the Arabian Sea. There, he would take his salt.

Dandi was about 240 miles (385 km) away, and the entire march took 25 days. The whole country followed its progress.

PACKING LIGHT

Gandhi did not take much with him on his march to the sea. He carried a bag that contained some rolled-up bedding, extra clothes, a mug, a diary, and a small, handheld spinning wheel.

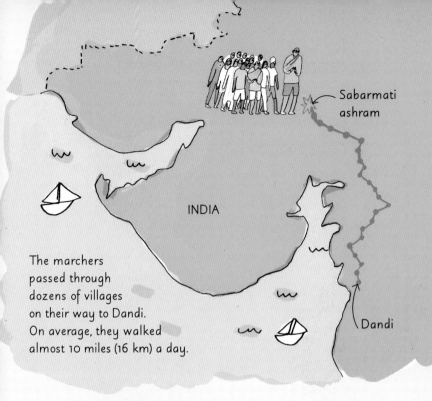

Sabarmati
ashram

INDIA

The marchers
passed through
dozens of villages
on their way to Dandi.
On average, they walked
almost 10 miles (16 km) a day.

Dandi

When Gandhi's group passed through a village, the townspeople came out to cheer them on. Each night, they found places where they were welcomed with food and somewhere to sleep. Gandhi gave speeches along the way, and he got up at 3 or 4 a.m. to write letters and articles. As they got nearer to Dandi, thousands of followers joined the march. Gandhi had the whole world's attention now. Journalists from all over had come to see what would happen.

On April 6, Gandhi performed his simple act. He walked into the waters of the Arabian Sea. Then he reached down and scooped up a nugget of salt from the mud. With that, he had broken the law—and everyone had seen him do it. The government wouldn't arrest him with everyone watching, but Gandhi knew it wouldn't be long.

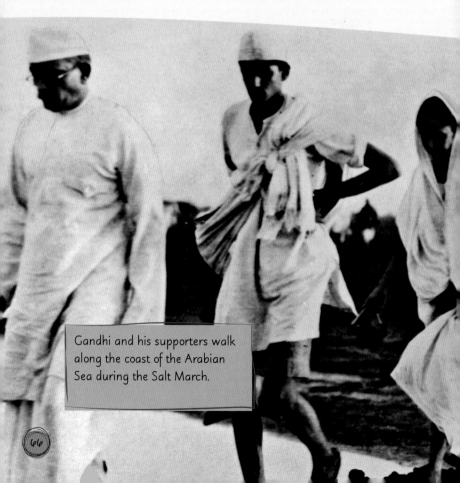

Gandhi and his supporters walk along the coast of the Arabian Sea during the Salt March.

Gandhi was the first to defy the British in this way, but thousands of others soon followed. All over the country, the people of India began collecting their own salt. Some took it out of the sea, like Gandhi had. Others got it from the earth. Selling illegal salt became a booming business in the cities. The pinch of salt Gandhi had taken from the sea was sold in an auction.

The winner of the auction paid 1,600 rupees, which would have a value of about $7,500 today.

The British pushed back against the illegal salt activity by arresting tens of thousands of people.

Gandhi was soon arrested, too. A month after the march, a British police officer came to Gandhi's camp late at night. He shone his flashlight in Gandhi's face to wake him up.

Gandhi had expected to be arrested, of course. It was what he had planned for. But before being led away, Gandhi asked for one small favor, which the police officer granted: He could brush his teeth first.

---

what is an auction?

A sale where people compete with one another to buy a particular item.

Gandhi speaks to a crowd in March 1930. People often gathered to hear Gandhi's inspirational words.

Gandhi leads a group of people during the Salt March.

Chapter 9

UNDER THE **mango** tree

Gandhi fasted and almost died to protest treatment of the untouchables. He was willing to do anything in his work for them.

In the eyes of the law, Gandhi was a criminal, but in the eyes of millions of Indians, he was a hero. British officials knew that sending him to jail made them look bad. Keeping him there made them look even worse, so they released him in early 1931.

Soon after, a journalist interviewed Gandhi. The journalist asked if Gandhi thought the Salt March would convince Britain to grant India independence. Gandhi said he didn't know. "But you are hopeful?" the journalist asked. "I am an optimist," Gandhi said.

---

what is an optimist?   Someone who looks on the bright side and does not focus on the negative.

Gandhi poses for a picture in London. He traveled there to discuss India's independence in 1931.

The journalist wanted to know something else: If Britain did not give India freedom, was Gandhi prepared to return to jail? "I am always prepared to return to jail," Gandhi replied with a chuckle.

In the summer of 1931, Gandhi traveled to Britain to talk about independence. It had been 40 years since Gandhi had been to England as a student. Now he was famous! He got his picture taken everywhere he went. Just like in India, the working people of England loved him.

However, the visit didn't really change anything. Things in India were about the same as they'd always been. Nothing was happening fast enough. When Gandhi got back home, he announced that he was ready to start another campaign of civil disobedience. British officials could not ignore that threat. Gandhi had told the journalist he was always prepared to return to jail, and that's exactly where he went.

On his 1931 trip to Britain, Gandhi was supplied with goats for their milk. By his side is his devoted supporter Madeleine Slade.

Gandhi enjoys meeting textile workers
while in Britain in September 1931.

Gandhi was in prison when he found out about another plan the British had. They were making small steps to give Indians more power, and one was to offer them more representatives in the government. That part was good. However, there would be a separate category for untouchables. To Gandhi, that part was bad. He did not want the untouchables to be singled out—and he was willing to prove it.

If the British followed through, Gandhi promised to start a fast. He would not eat until the British gave in, or until he died. In September 1932, he kept his word. He went out to the prison courtyard, laid down under a mango tree, and began his fast.

Gandhi had fasted before, but this time was worse. After a week, he was so weak that he was near death. British officials were nervous. In their scramble to make Gandhi happy, they offered a compromise. The untouchables would still be separate in the government, but they would get more seats. Gandhi accepted the deal. Everyone sighed with relief when he drank a sip of orange juice to end his fast.

Once again, Gandhi's actions had gotten a lot of attention. For a while, people treated the untouchables better. Usually they were not allowed to go into temples or to drink from public wells. Now they could. It didn't

A WAY OUT

Hindus believe that when a person dies, their soul can come back in the future in a new person's body. Hindus thought untouchables were people whose souls were being punished because they had done bad things in an earlier life. Some untouchables felt so desperate about their situation that they converted to another religion, where they were not shunned.

last long, though. Soon things were back to the old way. Gandhi decided he needed to do more.

In May 1933, he went back to his spot under the mango tree. He started a fast that lasted three weeks! Another fast came in August. By now, Gandhi was very sick and weak. If he kept fasting, he would surely die soon. Once again, the British let him out of jail. Gandhi faced a choice. If he went back to civil disobedience, he would just end up in prison again. That would make it harder to do his work. Instead, he went on a 12,000-mile (20,000-km) tour of the country to try to help the untouchables. When he traveled, people came from all over to see him. If they could get close enough, they could listen to him speak or even touch him.

WHOSE FAULT?

During Gandhi's tour of the country to help the untouchables, a huge earthquake hit the region of Bihar, India. Gandhi said it was God's punishment to Indians for treating untouchables so badly. A lot of people just believed the earthquake was a terrible tragedy. They were angry that Gandhi blamed them.

But most were content just to get a glimpse of the famous Mahatma.

Although Gandhi was loved by India's people, he knew he did not have as much political power as before. He used to have a lot of control over the Indian National Congress. Now the Congress had gone in another direction. Gandhi could not bring the changes he wanted. Frustrated, he wrote, "I have become helpless."

But he would not stay that way.

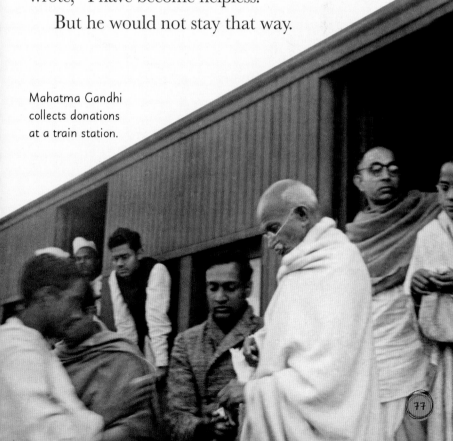

Mahatma Gandhi collects donations at a train station.

10

Vision FOR India

**With the start of World War II, India's
independence was closer than ever, but
Gandhi's dream of a united India was at risk.**

In the late 1930s, many countries in Europe
went to war again. Eventually Japan and the
United States got involved in it, too. Britain was
at the center of it all. The country was desperate
for people and other resources, such as food and
weapons, to help with the war effort. India was
one of the first places they turned.

Britain did not ask the people of India if
they wanted to get involved in the war effort.
Instead, they just dragged them into it. People
all over India were angry about that. Many
Indians felt the issues of World War II had
nothing to do with them. Why should they risk
their lives fighting for the British?

WORLD WAR II

In the 1930s, the German dictator Adolf Hitler rose to power. He had dreams of making Germans the most powerful people in the world, and he believed he could simply take what he wanted. In 1939, the German army invaded the neighboring country of Poland. Shocked into action, other European countries realized they had to stop Hitler, and World War II began. On one side were the Allied powers, which included Britain, France, Russia, China, and the United States. They fought against the Axis powers of Germany, Italy, and Japan. The war lasted until 1945, when the Allies won.

DID YOU KNOW?

Gandhi wrote a letter to Adolf Hitler, begging him not to go to war. Hitler never wrote back.

On the other hand, maybe the war could be a way to finally get independence. Indians could help Britain in the war, and in return, they could demand their freedom. Gandhi did not like the idea of trying to use the war against the British. That was not an honorable way to do things. Plus, he opposed war in general because it went against his belief in non-violence. Other political leaders in India saw it as an opportunity, however, and they wanted to take advantage of it.

Unsurprisingly the British did not like India making demands of them. For decades, the British had used Muslims and Hindus against each other. It helped them stay in control. They did the same thing now.

The Indian National Congress was mostly made up of Hindus. Britain told the Congress they expected help in the war, and if they did not get it, they would give more power to Muslims. That would cause even more tension in the country.

Hindus and Muslims already had different ideas of what the country should look like after independence. Gandhi's dream was of a single, united India. He knew the nation's people belonged to hundreds of different ethnic groups and spoke dozens of different languages. Of course, there were religious differences, too. Still, all of these people were Indians. Gandhi wanted them to come together. He believed that unity would be their greatest strength.

However, Muslims were nervous that Hindus had too much power. They wanted to split India into two nations. The "old" India

Sir Stafford Cripps, a British official, meets with Gandhi to discuss independence and the war in April 1942.

would be for Hindus. A new nation, called
Pakistan, would be for Muslims. Gandhi hated
this idea of partition. It went against so much
he had worked for.

In 1942, the British sent officials to India
to make a deal. One requirement was that
India had to cooperate with Britain during
the war. After that, India could become
independent.

It wasn't quite as simple as it seemed. The
offer also said that if any part of India wanted
to break off and go its own way, it would be
free to do so. That part of the offer worried
Gandhi, because it put his idea of "one India"
in danger.

Most Indians didn't like the deal anyway.
Nothing would happen until after the war,
and the British could just back out then.
India wanted action and independence now.
The British deal was rejected.

**what is
partition?**   The act of something being divided
into two or more parts.

With Gandhi's encouragement, the Indian National Congress went back to an older strategy: non-cooperation. Gandhi gave an inspiring speech to the Congress, in which he told them it was a "do or die" situation.

His words directly defied the British. He was arrested the next day, as was his wife, Kasturba, as well as most of the other leaders in the Congress. But the movement had started. Thousands of people marched in the streets demanding that the British "Quit India."

Protesters stand up to the government during the "Quit India" movement in 1942.

"We shall either **free India** or **die** in the attempt."

Gandhi,
August 8, 1942

85

DID YOU KNOW?

Kasturba was often affectionately called "Ba" by the Indian people. It means "mother."

Kasturba was put in the same prison as Gandhi, but she got sick soon afterward. Even though Gandhi tried to take care of her, she went steadily downhill. When she died in February 1944, Gandhi was by her side. They had been married for more than 60 years, and Gandhi was overcome with grief. "I cannot imagine life without Ba," he said.

The Indian people were passionate—and they were entirely fed up. Gandhi's hope of non-violent resistance, or satyagraha, fell apart. Angry Indians set fire to post offices and cut telephone lines. They destroyed bridges and railroads. Many people were killed, and a great many more were arrested.

Gandhi, stuck in prison, could only despair at what was happening in his beloved country.

The British had managed to stay in control for now, but it was clear that they were losing their grip. A few hundred thousand British could not control more than 300 million Indians for much longer.

Chapter 11

Independence

Gandhi did not like the way independence finally came to India, but he worked toward peace among all Indians until he died.

When Gandhi went to prison in 1942, he was used to being there, and the British were used to having him. However, Gandhi was older now, and prison was hard on him. Over the next two years, his health got much worse.

British officials faced the same problem they had in the past: If Gandhi died in prison, it could start an uncontrollable revolt across the country—and so, in May 1944, they released him.

World War II had been raging when Gandhi entered prison, and it was still going on when he got out. The question of India's independence had been pushed into the background.

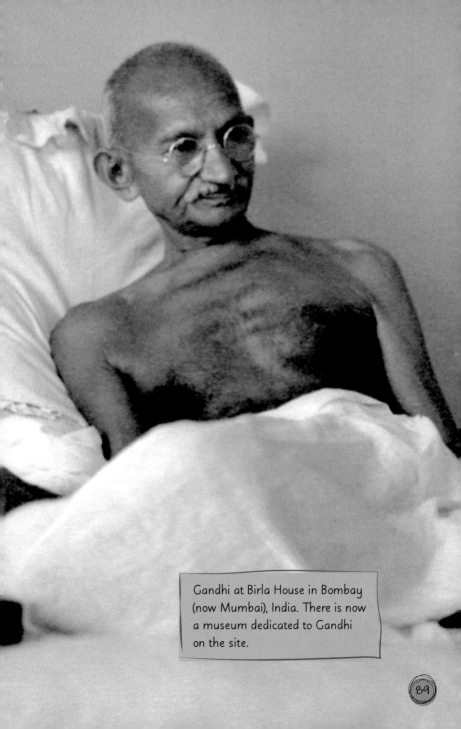

Gandhi at Birla House in Bombay (now Mumbai), India. There is now a museum dedicated to Gandhi on the site.

Peace came to Europe in September 1945 when the Allied powers won the war, but the situation in India was worse than ever. Muslims still wanted to create the state of Pakistan for themselves. The Indian National Congress was still against it.

In August 1946, Muslims declared a day of protest. It quickly got out of hand. Riots broke out as Muslims and Hindus attacked each other in the streets. The violence continued over the next few months, spreading through India.

Gandhi felt terrible about the violence. In a way, he felt it was his fault. Of course, he had not hurt anyone himself, but he felt it was his job to teach other people to be peaceful. In that respect, he had failed.

Gandhi traveled to villages all over India, offering whatever comfort he could. Sometimes he walked barefoot through filth and broken glass. It was his way of taking responsibility for his part in the trouble.

Clement Richard Attlee, prime minister of Britain from 1945 to 1951

By early 1947, the British were finally ready to make their move. The country had a new prime minister, Clement Richard Attlee, who was in favor of Indian independence. In March 1947, the prime minister sent someone over to work it out. His instructions were clear: This time, make it happen.

Gandhi still opposed the idea of two states, India and Pakistan, but he was caught in the middle. He had made enemies among Muslims. They thought he was trying to block them from having their own state. He had also made enemies of strict Hindus. They thought he was trying too hard to help Muslims instead of his own people. In their eyes, Gandhi was hurting India and her people.

Gandhi's idea of a peaceful compromise wasn't working. He couldn't win no matter what he did.

In the end, Britain agreed to the Muslims' demands to create Pakistan. Britain needed to get out of India, and this was the way to do it. Independence for two different nations was better than none at all.

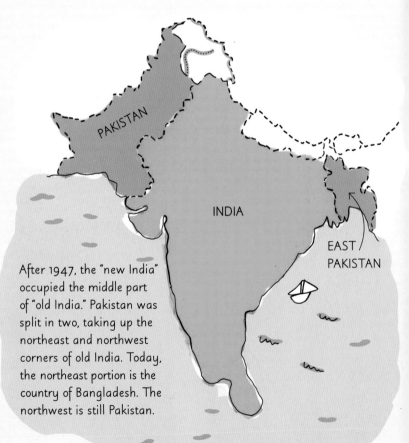

PAKISTAN

INDIA

EAST PAKISTAN

After 1947, the "new India" occupied the middle part of "old India." Pakistan was split in two, taking up the northeast and northwest corners of old India. Today, the northeast portion is the country of Bangladesh. The northwest is still Pakistan.

FLAG FOR THE NATION

An original design of India's flag had a spinning wheel in the center, to honor Gandhi's symbol of the nation. Later it was changed to the Wheel of Ashoka, or the "wheel of law," which stands for the belief that movement and growth are important in life. India's flag is required by law to be made from khadi, just as Gandhi would have wanted.

The details were arranged quickly. After decades of working for Indian independence, it finally came on August 15, 1947.

It did not happen the way Gandhi had wanted. He knew he had to accept it, but he felt discouraged. The creation of two states caused even more trouble. More than fifteen million people had to move from their homes. Muslims traveled to Pakistan; Hindus went to India. It was the largest migration of people in history.

What is migration? The act of moving from one place to another, usually in large numbers.

Trains were overcrowded with people moving to their new homes after the partition.

However, it was also terribly violent, with people attacking one another along the way. Gandhi fasted to try to bring peace between Hindus and Muslims, but while some people got his message, others did not want to hear it. Some people blamed Gandhi for sticking up for Muslims and not doing more to promote Hindus. One of those people was a man named Nathuram Godse.

On January 30, 1948, Gandhi was walking to get to his evening prayers. Suddenly Godse pushed his way through the crowd. Before anyone knew what was happening, Godse shot Gandhi three times. The Mahatma fell to the ground, dead at the age of 78. A life spent working for non-violence had ended with his assassination.

DID YOU KNOW?

More than one million people died during the violence of the Indian partition.

what is assassination?

To be killed because of political beliefs or actions.

As he died that day, Gandhi is said to have called out the words "Hey, Ram," which means "Oh, God."

Gandhi did not fear death. When the time came, he wanted to accept the spirit of God. Earlier in his life, Gandhi had once said, "If it occurs to me to utter the name of [God] with my last breath, it should be taken as proof [that I succeeded]."

The first prime minister of India, Jawaharlal Nehru, speaks to the newly independent country in 1947.

On August 18, 1947, the Indian flag is carried through the streets to celebrate the first Indian Independence Day.

12

A **lasting** impact

Decades after Gandhi's death, his message of peace lives on. Many leaders all over the world still try to follow in his footsteps.

When the new prime minister of India, Jawaharlal Nehru, heard that Gandhi had been killed, he was devastated. Nehru believed deeply in Gandhi. The two men had been friends for more than 30 years. Speaking to the Indian people on the radio, he said, "The light has gone out of our lives and there is darkness everywhere. Our beloved leader . . . is no more."

Nehru was 29 years old when he first met Gandhi. The two became close friends

Jawaharlal Nehru

and stayed that way until Gandhi's death. After India became independent, Nehru was elected the new country's first prime minister. His daughter, Indira Gandhi (not related to Mohandas Gandhi), later served two terms as prime minister.

Indira Gandhi

The next day, Gandhi was carried in a 5-mile (8-km) walk through the streets as more than two million people looked on and tossed flowers. Then a large pyre was built, and his body was cremated in the Hindu tradition. His ashes were scattered into the river to return his body to the world.

Even though Gandhi's life was over, his influence was still strong. Although some of his political opponents did not mourn his death, there were far more people who did. India's hero was dead. His cheerful smile and soft voice were gone, but the importance of his work was clearer than ever.

More than two million
people, including many
world leaders, attended
Gandhi's funeral
procession in 1948.

Gandhi had lived for almost 80 years. He had worked on three continents, and he had done incredible things. Through his leadership, India had finally achieved its independence. People called him the "Father of a Nation."

After the British "quit India," India became a democracy, which is a place where the people elect their government. India was the world's largest, simply because so many people lived there. Because of Gandhi's work, more people had a voice. There were important steps made toward treating everybody fairly. Gandhi had worked for years to help the untouchables. In 1950, India wrote a new constitution that made it illegal to discriminate against them.

CONSTITUTION OF INDIA

India's new constitution took three years to write. It is the longest one in the world! It borrowed ideas from the constitutions of several other countries—including France, Japan, and Ireland—and gave Indians more rights than they had ever had before.

Gandhi had always worked toward his goals with a spirit of peace. "There are many causes for which I am prepared to die," he once said, "but none for which I am prepared to kill." In the years after his death, many others tried to follow his ways.

Nelson Mandela named Gandhi as one of his strongest inspirations. Mandela was a political leader in South Africa, where Gandhi had spent his early life. He fought against South Africa's system of apartheid, which discriminated against black people. He wanted native Africans to be treated fairly and spent 27 years in jail because of his work. After he got out, he was elected president of South Africa in 1994. He was the country's first black president.

Nelson Mandela

The famous civil rights leader Dr. Martin Luther King Jr. was also inspired by Gandhi. King fought for equal rights for African-Americans during the Civil Rights Movement of the 1950s and 60s. Like Gandhi, he encouraged his supporters to protest without becoming violent. King often referred to Gandhi in his speeches and books. In a speech called "The Birth of a New Nation," King had said that without Gandhi and his followers, "India would have never been free." Both Gandhi and King worked tirelessly to improve the lives of people in need.

DID YOU KNOW?

In 1959, Dr. Martin Luther King Jr. went to India to learn more about Gandhi's life and teachings.

Dr. Martin Luther King Jr.

"If there had **not been** a Gandhi in India with all of his noble followers, **India** would have **never been free."**

Dr. Martin
Luther King Jr.,
1957

"[Gandhi] is a hero not just
to India, but to the world."
–Barack Obama, 2010

"Gandhi's views were the most
enlightened of all the political
men of our time."
–Albert Einstein, 1950

"Gandhi demonstrated that we
can force change and justice
through moral acts . . ."
–Steve Jobs, 1999

Many other notable people have also praised Gandhi's work—people such as Albert Einstein, a brilliant scientist who lived at the same time as Gandhi; Steve Jobs, who helped start the hugely successful company Apple; and Barack Obama, the first black president of the United States. Each of these people made important contributions to society, and they all spoke of Gandhi as a hero for human rights who had helped lead the way.

During his life, Mahatma Gandhi had many successes and just as many failures. His protests, fasts, marches, and speeches were milestones both in his life and in India's history. His actions touched millions of people and changed the lives of many, but his life was not just what he did for other people. It was also how he lived himself. Even during his quieter moments,

DID YOU KNOW?

Gandhi wrote a lot during his lifetime. Put together, his writings fill up almost 100 volumes!

when he wasn't surrounded by crowds, Gandhi
stood firm on his message. Change, he said,
really could happen with peace and love.

Gandhi always used his strengths, and
he always admitted his weaknesses. He never
tried to be perfect. He only tried to be the best
person he could be. In doing so, he showed
how one person can change the world.

The Mahatma Gandhi
statue in Washington, D.C.

109

Gandhi's
family tree

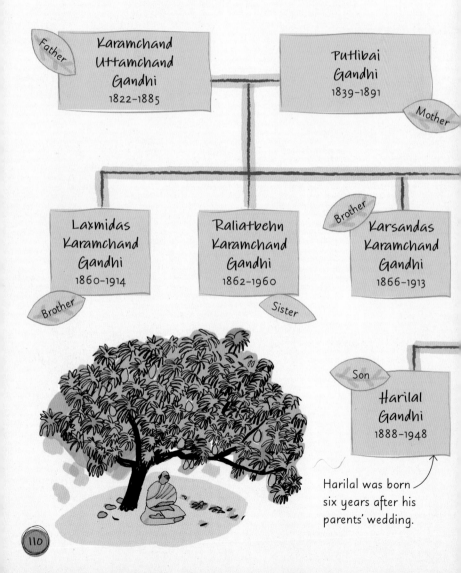

Mohandas Karamchand Gandhi was the youngest of his parents' four children.

Gandhi married Kasturba in 1883.

Mohandas Karamchand Gandhi

1869–1948

Wife

Kasturba Gandhi

1869–1944

Son

Son

Manilal Gandhi

1892–1956

Son

Ramdas Gandhi

1897–1969

Devdas Gandhi

1900–1957

Devdas was the youngest of his parents' four children, just like his father.

Timeline

Mohandas Karamchand
Gandhi is born in
Porbandar, India,
on October 2.

Gandhi helps found the
Natal Indian Congress
in South Africa.

Gandhi sails to
England to study law.

1869   1883   1888   1893   1894

Thirteen-year-old
Gandhi marries
Kasturba Kapadia.

Gandhi sails to South Africa
for work. He experiences
racial discrimination and
decides to protest against it.

Gandhi establishes the *Indian Opinion*, a newspaper for Indians, in South Africa.

Gandhi returns to India and travels across the country. In the same year, he is given the title of "Mahatma."

1903   1906   1913   1915   1917

Gandhi uses the word "satyagraha" for the first time to describe his non-violent beliefs.

Gandhi leads thousands of striking coal miners on a march to protest against their unfair treatment.

Gandhi leads a campaign for the rights of indigo farmers in Champaran.

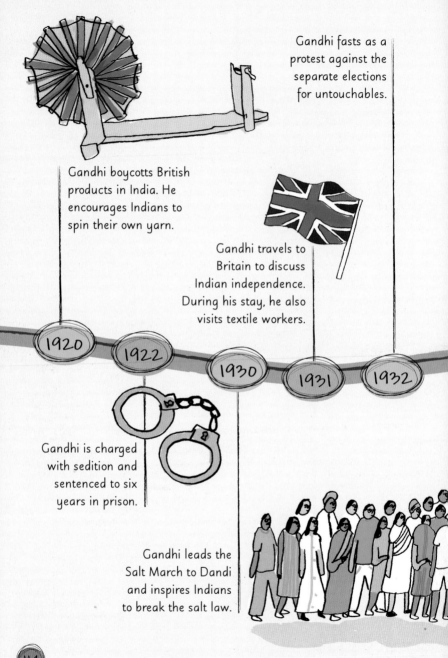

Gandhi fasts as a protest against the separate elections for untouchables.

Gandhi boycotts British products in India. He encourages Indians to spin their own yarn.

Gandhi travels to Britain to discuss Indian independence. During his stay, he also visits textile workers.

1920 1922 1930 1931 1932

Gandhi is charged with sedition and sentenced to six years in prison.

Gandhi leads the Salt March to Dandi and inspires Indians to break the salt law.

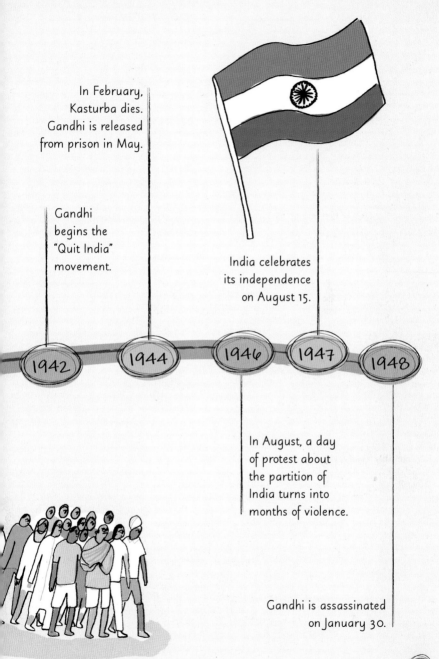

In February, Kasturba dies. Gandhi is released from prison in May.

Gandhi begins the "Quit India" movement.

India celebrates its independence on August 15.

1942   1944   1946   1947   1948

In August, a day of protest about the partition of India turns into months of violence.

Gandhi is assassinated on January 30.

Quiz

 1 Where was Mohandas Karamchand Gandhi born?

 2 What happened when Gandhi appeared in court as a lawyer for the first time?

 3 Which political group did Gandhi help form in South Africa?

 4 What word meaning "truth force" did Gandhi give to his philosophy of doing what's right?

 5 Which group of people did Gandhi visit in Champaran in 1917 in order to help them?

 6 What two professions did Gandhi write on his paperwork when he was arrested in 1922?

 7 On which day of the week did Gandhi refuse to talk unless it was urgent?

Do you remember what you've read? How many of these questions about Gandhi's life can you answer?

 How many days did it take Gandhi and his followers to complete the Salt March?

 Under which type of tree did Gandhi fast while in prison?

 What does Kasturba's nickname, "Ba," mean?

 How many people moved from their homes during the Indian partition?

 What 1950 document made it illegal to discriminate against the untouchables?

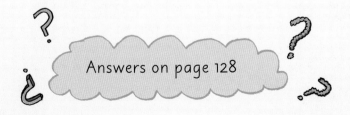
Answers on page 128

Who's who?

Attlee, Clement Richard
(1883–1967) British prime minister from 1945 to 1951

Cripps, Sir Stafford
(1889–1952) chief finance minister of Britain from 1947 to 1950; met with Gandhi to discuss Indian independence in 1942

Einstein, Albert
(1879–1955) German-born physicist and Nobel Prize winner for his work in the field of theoretical physics

Gandhi, Harilal
(1888–1948) oldest of Gandhi's four sons

Gandhi, Indira
(1917–1984) prime minister of India from 1966 to 1977, and again from 1980 to 1984; India's first woman prime minister

Gandhi, Karamchand Uttamchand
(1822–1885) Gandhi's father

Gandhi, Karsandas Karamchand
(1866–1913) Gandhi's older brother

Gandhi, Kasturba
(1869–1944) Gandhi's wife; affectionately called "Ba," which means "mother," by the people of India

Gandhi, Laxmidas Karamchand
(1860–1914) Gandhi's oldest brother

Gandhi, Manilal
(1892–1956) Gandhi's second-oldest son

Gandhi, Putlibai
(1839–1891) Gandhi's mother

Gandhi, Raliatbehn Karamchand
(1862–1960) Gandhi's sister

Godse, Nathuram
(1910–1949) man who
assassinated Gandhi

Hitler, Adolf
(1889–1945) chancellor
of Germany during World
War II and leader of the
Nazi Party

Jobs, Steve
(1955–2011) inventor,
designer, and entrepreneur
who helped found the Apple
computer company

King Jr., Martin Luther
(1929–1968) activist and
public speaker who led the
Civil Rights Movement in
the United States in the
1950s and 60s

Mandela, Nelson
(1918–2013) president of
South Africa from 1994 to
1999; South Africa's first
black president

Nehru, Jawaharlal
(1889–1964) prime minster
of India from 1947 to
1964; India's first prime
minister after it became
an independent nation

Obama, Barack
(1961–) president of the
United States from 2009 to
2017; America's first black
president

Slade, Madeleine
(1892–1982) one of
Gandhi's most dedicated
followers; left her home in
Britain to live with and
learn from Gandhi

Glossary

ahimsa
ancient Hindu belief that people should not behave violently

ashram
farm or settlement where people with the same spiritual beliefs live together

assassination
when someone is killed due to his or her political beliefs or actions

auction
sale in which people compete with one another to buy a particular item

boycott
refusing to buy products or use the services of a company or government, usually as a form of political protest

caste
in the Hindu religion, a group that people are born into

civil disobedience
using peaceful methods when refusing to follow laws believed to be unfair

constitution
document listing the rights of a nation's citizens and how its goverment should work

cremation
burning a body after death; the ashes may be saved or disposed of in a ceremony

democracy
government in which people elect their leaders

dhoti
traditional item of clothing for Hindu men that is made of a piece of cloth wrapped and tied around the waist

fast
act of not eating for a period of time, sometimes as a form of protest

hartal
Hindu word for going on strike against an employer or the government

Hindu
person who follows Hinduism, the largest religion in India

home rule
government of a nation by its own people while still being a colony, or under the control, of another country

hunger strike
when a prisoner refuses to eat as a protest

immigrant
someone who moves from their home country to another one

independence
when a country is no longer part of, or governed by, another country

khadi
Indian cloth that
is woven at home

Mahatma
title of great respect,
given to Gandhi,
meaning "great soul"

martyr
person whose death
inspires others to fight
for their cause

migration
act of moving
from one place to
another, usually in
large numbers

Muslim
follower of the
religion Islam

non-cooperation
peacefully protesting
British rule in India
without breaking the law,
such as by boycotting
British goods and schools

optimist
someone who looks
on the bright side
and does not focus
on the negative

partition
act of something being
divided into two or
more parts

prejudice
having opinions, usually
bad, about people and
without good reason

protest
to show that you
disapprove of, or do not
agree with, something

pyre
structure or heap,
usually made of wood,
for cremating, or
burning a dead body

salt flats
crusty layers of salt
that form gradually
where ocean tides
wash up on beaches

satyagraha
non-violent political
struggle

sedition
act of working against
or trying to overthrow
a government

strike
when workers refuse
to work in order to
convince or force
their employer to
meet their demands

temple
place for religious
worship

turban
headdress made from
a long cloth wrapped
around the head

untouchable
person considered to
have no status in the
Indian caste system

Index

Acknowledgments

DK would like to thank: Romi Chakraborty and Pallavi Narain for design support; Maya Frank-Levine for proofreading; Helen Peters for the index; and Priti Mishra and Stephanie Laird for consulting.

The publisher would like to thank the following for their kind permission to reproduce their photographs:

(Key: a-above; b-below/bottom; c-center; f-far; l-left; r-right; t-top)

6 Alamy Stock Photo: Dinodia Photos (tr). 9 Photo Division Ministry of Information and Broadcasting. 10 Alamy Stock Photo: Dinodia Photos (tl). 11 Alamy Stock Photo: Dinodia Photos. 15 Alamy Stock Photo: Maurice Joseph. 16 Library of Congress, Washington, D.C.: LC-DIG-ppmsc-08560. 20 Alamy Stock Photo: Dinodia Photos. 22 Alamy Stock Photo: Dinodia Photos. 29 Alamy Stock Photo: Dinodia Photos. 31 Alamy Stock Photo: World History Archive. 36–37 Alamy Stock Photo: Dinodia Photos. 39 Alamy Stock Photo: Dinodia Photos (ca, cb). 41 Wellcome Images http://creativecommons.org/licenses/by/4.0/: Wellcome Collection. 47 Alamy Stock Photo: World History Archive. 51 Alamy Stock Photo: Chronicle. 55 Alamy Stock Photo: Dinodia Photos. 57 Alamy Stock Photo: The Print Collector. 62–63 Getty Images: Bettmann. 66–67 Getty Images: Time Life Pictures. 69 Alamy Stock Photo: Dinodia Photos (ca, cb). 71 Getty Images: ullstein bild Dtl.. 73 Alamy Stock Photo: Classic Image (ca); Dinodia Photos (cb). 77 Alamy Stock Photo: Dinodia Photos. 82 Alamy Stock Photo: Military History Collection. 84 Alamy Stock Photo: Dinodia Photos. 89 Alamy Stock Photo: Dinodia Photos. 91 Alamy Stock Photo: Keystone Pictures USA. 93 Dreamstime.com: Jayv. 94 Alamy Stock Photo: UtCon Collection. 97 Alamy Stock Photo: Historic Collection (ca); Keystone Pictures USA (cb). 98 Alamy Stock Photo: Everett Collection Historical. 99 Getty Images: Tim Graham (cra). 100–101 Getty Images: Haynes Archive / Popperfoto. 103 Alamy Stock Photo: Trinity Mirror / Mirrorpix. 104 Library of Congress, Washington, D.C.: LC-USZ62-126559. 106 Alamy Stock Photo: Allstar Picture Library (crb). Library of Congress, Washington, D.C.: (clb); LC-DIG-ppbd- 00358 (ca). 109 Alamy Stock Photo: Maurice Savage. 111 Alamy Stock Photo: World History Archive (ca)

Cover images: Front and Spine: Getty Images: Bettmann

All other images © Dorling Kindersley
For further information see: www.dkimages.com

ANSWERS TO THE QUIZ ON PAGES 116–117

1. Porbandar, India; 2. He became tongue-tied and could not speak; 3. Natal Indian Congress; 4. satyagraha; 5. indigo farmers; 6. farmer and weaver; 7. Monday; 8. 25 days; 9. mango tree; 10. mother; 11. more than 15 million people; 12. Constitution of India